Heart's E

By
Renetha Fenton

MAPLE
PUBLISHERS

Heart's Emotions

Author: Renetha Fenton

Copyright © Renetha Fenton (2024)

The right of Renetha Fenton to be identified as author of this work has been asserted by the author in accordance with section 77 and 78 of the Copyright, Designs and Patents Act 1988.

First Published in 2024

ISBN 978-1-83538-176-2 (Paperback)

Book cover design by:
Kush Turner

Published by:
Maple Publishers
Fairbourne Drive, Atterbury,
Milton Keynes,
MK10 9RG, UK
www.maplepublishers.com

A CIP catalogue record for this title is available from the British Library.

About the Author

The author was born in Antigua, the youngest of fourteen children. She is married with five children, one girl and four boys. Unfortunately, two of her boys have passed on to glory.

She finds lessons and inspiration from her circumstances. Not much of a talker, she expresses herself through writing.

Dedication

This book is dedicated to my children.

Acknowledgments

I should like to thank the people for their support and encouragement while I was writing this book, especially: Gilbert Daley, Gert Daley, Nicole Fergus, Anisha Fernandez and Blossome Daley.

Life can be very difficult at times, but being home alone can be an inspiration to a lot of things. It gives you the opportunity to sort out your distraught, difficult and complicated life. You can become a doctor, lawyer or police officer, rather than being a lonely housewife. This book consists of things that happen in everyday life. The names mentioned in the poems are pure inventions.

A WALK IN THE PARK

It was getting very dark.
However, I continued on my walk through Boxtree Park.
My headache got more severe and my eyes began to get dark.
I stumbled and collapsed on the path.
I tried to reach the bench that was a few feet in front of me
But I was unable to move and could hardly see.

I shouted for help but did not make much of a sound.
Intensely I listened but it did not seem as if anyone was around.
I was completely helpless and I did not know why.
The pain was intense and tears flowed from my eyes.
My heart was filled with so much sadness
It felt as heavy as lead.

I laid there in what seemed to be a puddle
I was desperate for even a little cuddle.
I was completely terrified
And thought I was going to die.
I went earnestly to God in prayer
Because I did not want to die at least not out here.
I was conscious of my situation
And knew that I needed immediate attention.

Then I heard voices that sounded very near
And I thanked God for his quick respond to my prayer.
It did seem like an eternity
Before someone came and rescued me.

I was not conscious of what happened next
But when I regain consciousness
I was in a hospital bed
With a bandage wrapped around my head.
The Tumour was gone
Unfortunately, so was my sight.
But with God, I decided to put things right.

Although I would be living in a world of darkness,
I had regained my voice and was no longer motionless.
I could have died right there and then
But I was given another chance to repent.
Today I profess Christianity.
I will thank God continuously
For his goodness and mercy towards me.

WHY ME?

I was an athlete with good health and physique.
I went for a walk to stretch my legs
And relax my brain from all the stress.
Suddenly I became helpless.
Why did it happen to me Lord?
Why, why oh Lord why me?

I could not walk and I could not talk,
But why could I not I see?
Why could I not reach home
Where I would be in someone's care?
Or why could I not at least reach on the bench that was near?
Why did it happen in such cold atmosphere?
Why did it happen to me Lord?
Why, why oh Lord why me?

I had just begun to live my life aiming towards my goals
And reaching for higher heights.
Unfortunately, I lost my sight.
What had I done to deserve such punishment?
What had I done?
Why did all these things happen to me Lord?
Why, why oh Lord why me?

More and more questions were floating around
And there were no answers to be found.
What I cannot understand Lord is why can I not see?

And why me?
Why did it happen to me Lord?
Why, why oh Lord why me?

THANK GOD

I came very close to death
But it was not my time as yet.
For I had a miraculous recovery
But physically I still could not see.
However, God's face shone as a light before me,
And as I live from day to day,
I will continue to praise him without delay.

Thank God my life did not end
I thank him for my family and friends.
Thank God for the people who found me
Father bless them abundantly.
Thank God for the doctors and nurses
who helped me to revive.
Thank God for another chance of being a mother and a wife.
Most of all, thank God for sparing my life.

GOD ANSWERS PRAYER

When nothing is in your house to eat,
Not a crumb or a piece of meat,
For church you have a few dresses and a pair of shoes.
Are you worried over these earthly events?
Loved ones have no fear.
Just talk to God in prayer.

Whenever it seems impossible to live
from one day to the next,
Remember God promised he will
supply our every need.
When trials and temptation come your way
My dear just continue to pray.

When you are pressured by your foes
And you wonder where else to turn,
Let your faith begin to rise.
Believe in your Saviour.
Because my dear,
He will answer your prayer.

THE ROCK AND THE SAND

Jesus is the rock, the Devil is the sand.
Who is holding your hand?
Reach for the rock, not to the sand,
For he will never let go of your hand.

If you hold on to the sand
And find that you are sinking,
Remember Jesus is patiently waiting!
Get out while you can
And reach for his unchanging hand.
He will never forsake you
But gladly, receive you.

When you hold on to the rock
You will find love, joy and peace
Then the Devil will not be able to defeat you.
But if you let go of Jesus' hand
You will fall into the sand
And eternally acknowledge the Devil's command.

THE WIND

The wind is something that cannot be seen.
It is like the spirit of God that dwells within.
When it passes our way
Just thank God for another day.

Whenever the wind is blowing
It makes you feel cool and refreshed.
The gentle caress against one's face
Encourages thanksgiving for his Grace

Sometimes the wind is so calm,
Then suddenly it turns into a storm.
But if we trust God it will do no harm
For miracles He the Almighty can perform.

ADVICE TO MAN

Kingdoms rise and Kingdoms fall,
This my friends happens to one and all.
If at any time I scratch your back,
Remember someday to scratch mine back.

Be kind and fair to everyone,
Because someday you may need a helping hand.
Avoid hurting anyone
Whether or not they are in your care,
Especially if that person is blind or unable to hear.

Be friendly and respectful of everyone,
For this world is round not square.
Whatever evil you may have done
It will come back to hurt you and your loved ones.

Do unto others what you would like them to do unto you.
Give to them what you would take for you.
My friends be honest and do good not evil,
And do not let your life be control by the devil.

So reward a man honestly,
When he works hard to make a living.
Because sometimes the flesh is weak,
But the spirit is willing.
Give to him what is rightfully his
especially if he earns it with tears and sweat.

Wash your hands and keep them clean,
For there is only good and evil no in between.
My friends please take my advice,
Do not be foolish-be wise.

MY STEPFATHER

My stepfather was a child molester!
Whenever I told my mother about
the horrible things he did to me,
She did not accept the fact
That her husband was capable of such a criminal act.

For years I lived in fear and agony,
As my stepfather continued to sexually molest me.
The result was a baby.
My mother did not believe me when I told her,
that her husband was my child's father.

Because my mother was a Christian,
And her husband was well respected
in the community,
They did not want me to have an abortion.
But arranged for me to give the child up for adoption.

I hated my stepfather for what he had done to me,
Especially when I think of my baby.
My dear Jessica wherever you may be,
I pray you may never experience what happened to me.

THE LAWYER

My mother got pregnant by her stepfather,
And I was the result of that disaster.
But the wealthy family who adopted me,
Loved and cared for me dearly.

When I learned that I had been conceived
by such a criminal act,
I was embarrassed and did not want to accept the fact.
I forgave my mother for giving me up for adoption,
Because I believed she made the right decision.

I have put the past behind me
And have worked hard to go to university.
My goal was to become a lawyer,
To defend people who were abused like my mother.

However I was conceived,
I thank God for the things I have achieved.
Such as my diploma from college
My law degree from university
And the darn fine lawyer that I turned out to be.

MOTHER

In the coffin she lay showing only her beautiful face
I looked at her and whispered a little grace
As the tears ran down my worried face.
I woke up with a headache and dark circles under my eyes
For it was my mother who had died.
I lay dumfounded on the bed
And realised that she was already dead.

Mother, Oh mother! I wish that you could return from the dead
For there are so many things that were left unsaid.
I knew you went through a lot of suffering and pain,
But how I wished that I could hear your lovely voice again.
Even if it is a complain.
I often felt your presence near,
Each time I called your name in prayer.

LACK OF ATTENTION

My mother died when I was a youngster.
Oh, how I wished that I had a brother or a sister!
My father who was an alcoholic
Did not pay me much attention,
And I didn't know how to cope with the situation
So I turned to alcohol for solace and comfort.

However, I was more fortunate than my father
For he had died three years later.
I drank so much alcohol that a flicker from a lighter,
would have probably set me on fire.
But the alcohol could not fulfil my emptiness,
So I gave it a permanent rest.

A few years later I was introduced to a drug called cocaine;
That I would not like to experience again.
I was scared to death
When I saw that the blood from my nose
Made a huge patch on the bed.
I realised then that my life could suddenly come to an end,
And I wished that I hadn't accepted the drug from my friend.

I wanted something to relieve the stress,
I didn't expect the drug to have such deadly effects.
It had almost destroyed my life.
However, I thank God each day for the chance
To be a mother and a wife.

DO NOT REPEAT IT

If your parents are abusive or use drugs;
Whether it is alcohol cannabis or cocaine,
Please do not do the same.
These drugs will damage your brain.
You may even end up dead or insane.
You may be their child
But you can also be a mentor and a good friend.
Encourage them to bring the drugs
And abusiveness to an end.

Be bold and set yourself a goal.
Respect your parents
And listen carefully to what you are told.
Stand up for your rights
Say no to drugs and fight the good fight.
Do not hate your parents
For whatever wrong they may have done,
For each of us have erred and strayed.
And it will take much prayer and willpower,
To break generational curses sent forth
To destroy you and your family.

PROMISES

When Hurricane Hugo pass in 1989,
Fear gripped the peoples' hearts
As it ripped their little Island apart.
Homeless, clothesless and foodless
They struggled to survive
And thanked God for sparing their lives.
Many accepted him as their Saviour
But soon they forgot about him, the creator.
As the country got back on its feet
The people became careless, fearless and indiscreet.

Then the volcano began to rumble!
And again fear welled up in the hearts of the people.
They had barely recovered from the previous disaster
And were horrified as they faced another.
But was this a message from the heavenly father?

When the earth trembled from the impact of an eruption,
The ash ascended as the pyroclastic flow descended.
It took everything that was in its path,
Fear intensified the peoples' minds and hearts.
To God they earnestly went in prayer,
Seeking his forgiveness with tears.

The volcano has been active for years
And has been the peoples' worse nightmare.
They were in a disastrous situation
So the government had to make some quick and difficult
decisions.

One third of the Island was declared an exclusion zone,
And two third of the population fled the Island
Seeking a more peaceful home.

THE VOLCANO

Montserrat is thirty-nine square miles of beautiful gem,
With hill, valleys, mountains and beaches with black sand.
Its highest mountain is Chances Peak,
But the volcano destroyed its beauty that was so sweet.
Many hurricanes have also damaged it on their way
But the volcano looks like it is here to stay.

Often the people were afraid to sleep,
For they did not know when the alarm was going to beep.
The pyroclastic flows were so sneaky,
They crept up on villagers unexpectedly.
When a pyroclastic flow raced through Long Ground,
All of the villagers had to run into town.

Schools and churches were filled with people who relocated
From the volcano that tried to take their lives.
Sometimes when the volcano erupted it got so dark
People could not even see where to walk.
Parents screamed, children cried
And each wondered if they were going to survive.

Three years had passed since the volcano started to erupt,
Yet it does not seem as if it is going to stop.
Islanders who could not cope with the situation
Went abroad to better their condition
But many found themselves in a more difficult position.

THE ASH AND THE SNOW

Montserratians who went to England did not consider
The situation of the country and its weather.
They thought that it was the best place to go,
So many migrated there because of the volcano.

There were many other Caribbean islands to which they
could go,
After they had lost their properties in the pyroclastic flow,
But they wanted to experience life in a country that had
snow.
They did not have much left to lose
So England was the country they chose.

They were given accommodation and financial benefits.
They thought Hey, why not sit back and enjoy it.
A few months later their allowance needed to increase,
Because of the temperature which plummeted to zero
degrees.

The Jobseeker's allowance was not enough;
Life for them became very rough.
They sought for work every day,
And often got lost along the way.
Some had experience and some had none,
All each wanted was to make some extra money.

Long hours of work and not enough rest,
Have caused them to become depressed.
Then they complained every day

About the house rent and council tax they had to pay.

They could not cope with the busy life of England,
So many returned to the Island they had abandoned.
To the land of ash and pyroclastic flow,
Because they prefer the ash to the snow.

PETITION DENIED

You left your country because of a disaster,
And went to Britain thinking life would be better.
There were no relatives over there to accommodate you,
And a friend offered you a room for a week or two.
Unfortunately, before the third day light
You became an obstacle in their sight.

A few days later they accompanied you
To the Housing Association,
And you were given temporary accommodation.
You had to share the room with your son,
It was not a very comfortable situation.
However, you wanted to learn your way about
So you decided to venture out.

The sun was shining beautifully
But the darn place was cold and windy.
One had never experienced anything like that,
Had to go back inside to put on a coat and a hat.
Everywhere looked confusing!
The directions were difficult to figure out
You could not tell if you were going
east, west, north or south.

Then a few weeks later you were moved
To a permanent accommodation.
It was more convenient that the previous one.
One year later when your other children decided to join you,
Each of the bedrooms had to be shared between two.

The apartment then became unsuitable accommodation
And you were left in a difficult situation.

You wrote to the Housing Association
requesting a larger accommodation.
Unfortunately, they turned down your petition
Stating that the apartment was a suitable one.
You were not comfortable with the fact
That they looked at the age gap
And not the actual age of the children,
Which they should have taken into consideration.

Tension grew between the children because of lack of
privacy.
You could not afford to rent a private property
And pay for your children's studies at college and university.
So, there you were stuck in the apartment
Because you wanted to stay together as a family.

LIVING IN ENGLAND

Living in England is very hard,
Making new decisions is only a part.
Plenty of tax for every man,
And very little money, for you to live on.

Living in England is no joy ride,
Men leave women, husbands leave wives.
Families are affected in everyday life,
Beating the system is the only choice.

Colder than ice is the winter time,
Man still works hard, even if he gets frost bite.
He drinks plenty of tea to keep some warmth inside,
But at the end of the week he breaks down and cries.

Three pounds sixty an hour to support children and wife,
So man works hard day and night.
With so many bills to pay,
Man's salary can only go half way.

Food and clothes he has to provide,
For him and his family to survive.
My friends take my advice,
Do not let the pressure of living in England
Make you commit suicide.

IN A FOUR ROOM HOUSE

On the door step of a four-room house,
Three little children sat as quiet as a mouse,
Each had a finger in his mouth.
It was their mother's washing day,
And they were tired of heading water
from a tap, quarter of a mile away.

When their chores and homework were done,
It was time for them to have some fun.
They all went to play
with their friends who lived at Crossway.

At the setting of the sun,
To their home they began to run.
To wash their hands and faces
in the basin of water that was there,
For they knew, that supper time was near.

They sat on the floor in a semi-circle,
And waited patiently, for their food that was on the table.
With legs crossed and hands clasped they said a prayer,
And thanked God for whatever food was there.

Supper was finished but it was not time for bed,
So they sat on the door step and waited for their father
instead.
They spotted him as he approached the foot path,
And with much love and joy in their heart,
They ran to meet him down the path.

One was on his back and at each side,
As he strode home with pride and joy in his eyes.
Their mum was at the door with a wide smile on her face.
She greeted her husband lovingly
Who came home from a hard day's work.

I HAVE NOT FORGOTTEN

Montserrat, Montserrat, beautiful Montserrat
the peaceful little Island that I cannot forget,
With pastures green, hills, mountains and valleys between.
The volcano destroyed most of the beauty that was there to
be seen.
Properties, lives and historical sites,
Were all shattered in a single swipe.

The glow from the volcano was a beautiful sight
Especially when I watched it at night.
But when I saw rocks of fire roll down the path,
Fear gripped my troubled heart.
I prayed earnestly to survive
Hoping to catch the very next flight.

I was extremely anxious to leave the country.
But, I had financial difficulty
and was stuck there indefinitely.
Whenever there was an eruption
and the earth trembled from the explosion
I was paralysed with fear,
As ash soared thousands of feet into the air.

When a major eruption destroyed the southern part of the
Island,
The government decided on an evacuation.
It was the perfect solution to my situation.
I finally got the chance to go and better my condition!
But I miss my little Island very much

Despite the fact that a part of it is now covered in ash.

I wish that I could go back
to my beautiful house that was upon the hill top.
However, that was not to be
As the volcano had destroyed my property.
But I will never forget
That beautiful little Island called Montserrat.

A MESSAGE

Many years ago, you told me that you were going to get
married.
Now that the time has finally come, I hope that it would be
solid.
Do not let your problems get you down.
Put a smile on your face and not a frown.

Try to stay as young and as healthy as you are.
Do not worry about building a house, or buying a car.
Be content with what you have got,
Because some people would be glad to have half as much as
that.
So my dear, count your blessings
And not what is missing.

A SPECIAL FRIEND

You are a very special friend
who will cheer me up when I'm sad,
The type of friend I never had.
Your smile always brightens my day
In a very special and friendly way.
I will miss you badly when you move away.

Some people will say out of sight out of mind
But please do not forget you will leave me behind.
My number is 0000,09.
You have promise to keep in touch,
And I am very grateful for even that much.

MY DEAR UNCLE

My dear uncle Ted I really do love you.
You were always there when I needed you.
You calmed me down when I was mad
And made me laugh when I was sad.

I miss you now that you have moved away
But I will come to visit you someday.
Was there not a place nearby that you could have moved to?
It was a great pleasure living next door to you.

Uncle Ted, Hemel Hempstead is so far.
Probably it would be best if I buy a car.
And whenever I need to,
I could just drive over to see you.

I LOVE YOU

You are my darling, you are my sweetheart.
I do not want us to be apart.
You are my soul, you are my life,
I would very much like to be your wife.
You are my lover, you are my husband to be.
It would be a pleasure for me to have your baby.

You are my heart, you are my everything
You are all the reason I need to keep me going.
I do not know what else to say or do
To prove my sincere love for you.
If you could ever get a glimpse inside of my heart,
You will find your name engraved on every part.

I MISS YOU

Relax my sweetheart I will be home soon.
It may even be tomorrow afternoon.
Memories will probably fill your thoughts,
Especially now that we are so far apart.
So may your heart be filled with gladness.
Give that beautiful body of yours some rest.
As the days go by I miss you so much,
I regret the day I left home in such a rush.

I do not like being away from you.
Leaving was a difficult thing for me to do.
On the days when I feel lonely,
I would very much like to be next to your body.
Especially when I remember
That day when you and I had a shower,
With our bodies soapy and drenched
Understanding how much we mean to each other.

WILL YOU MARRY ME?

I am handsome and healthy.
Unfortunately, I am not wealthy.
However, you have captured my heart.
A ring I would have bought if I could afford the money.
I love you honey.
Will you marry me?

Thanks for the flowers sweetheart,
I do love you with all my heart.
But, I hope that what I am about to say
Will not keep us apart.
I am a teenager and soon to be a mother.
You are asking me to commit to another.
I am sorry, but I cannot accept your proposal.
Will you wait until I am twenty-one?

My darling dear, you have broken my heart,
But I will not let that keep us apart.
It took me five years to reach this far
And another five will not be much of a matter.
We are together, and we love each other.

Thanks for understanding my darling,
I hope that by then, you can afford a ring.
But if you cannot I will understand,
Because I do want you to be my husband.

FIVE YEARS LATER

Honey, those five years went by very quickly.
However, I did manage to save some money.
Now that you are twenty-one,
Do you still want me to be your husband?

Sweetheart, that is a dumb question for you to ask.
Those five years of waiting were a very difficult task.
But I am ready and willing to walk down that aisle,
Even if I have to walk a mile.

MEMORIES

I watched you walk down the aisle
Wearing that lovely white dress and a beautiful smile.
You looked like an angel floating towards me,
And I felt like I was in heaven with all of its glory.
When you said, 'I do', in your sweet angelic voice,
I knew that I had made the right choice
When I asked you to be my wife.

When you first came into my life
My dream was to become your wife.
But I did not believe that you truly understand
When I asked you to wait until I was twenty-one.
I stood at the altar facing you
And was overwhelmed to know that my dream had come
true.
You are a very patient and special man
To have waited for me that long.
I am proud to have you as my husband!

WITHOUT YOU

You are my eyes,
Without you I am blind.
You are my ears,
Without you I am deaf.
You are my mouth,
Without you I am dumb.
You are my hands,
Without you they are useless.
You are my feet,
Without you they are motionless.
You are my heart,
Without you I will be dead.
You are my life and the only love I have got.
Without you I will be like a corpse
In a coffin waiting to be buried.

MY FIANCÉ

My fiancé promised to be home at three
So I sat on the sofa and waited patiently,
While I watched my favourite soap opera program on the
Television.
Suddenly there was a knock at the door.
When I looked at the clock, it was half past four.
I hoped that he did not lose the key,
For that was the only one left of three.
And he promised to cut another one for me.

Despite the fact that he was late,
I was glad that he was home and safe
For we were going to set our wedding date.
But when I open the door I saw two policemen.
One of them was Albert's best friend.
The neighbours all stood and stared
While I tried to figure out why the policemen were here.

Fear gripped my heart.
I tried very hard not to fall apart.
Shocked overwhelmed me by what one of the policemen
said
And I slumped lifelessly unto the sofa bed.
My fiancé was in a car accident about six blocks away
At the junction of Nugent Street and Crossway.

He was in a critical condition
At the St. Joseph Accident and Emergency Hospital.
He was unconscious when I got there,

So I went earnestly to God in prayer.
He looked like he was already dead,
As he lay there powerless on the bed.

About five hours later he regained consciousness,
And in a very faint whisper he said,
I love you Izamay.
And with that his life ebbed away.
I was devastated and wept helplessly,
for he was not only my fiancé,
But was also the father of my unborn baby.

BLINDED BY LOVE

I was blinded by love and desperate for stability,
When I fell in love with a fellow called Manny.
But over the years
I have shed many tears.
I've spent many lonely nights on my tear-stained pillow,
As I waited patiently for Manny, who seldom showed.
I trusted him implicitly,
But he was unfaithful to me.

I knew then that he had another lover.
However, I stayed in the relationship
Hoping that things would improve.
At my birthday party in Mill End,
I saw him making love with my best friend.
Piece by piece, my heart was stripped away
As I stood there and stared in dismay.

Day by day my life slowly fell apart,
And I knew from this relationship, I had to walk.
But, I was convinced by his apology
And got really excited when he proposed to me.
I felt so comfortable and secure,
I did not dare ask for anything more.
I was overwhelmed with joy,
When I had our beautiful baby boy.

However, I had the worse shock of my life
When Manny and Amy became husband and wife.
I was devastated and could not cope with the situation.

A suicide attempt was my final decision.
But thank God I had a miraculous recovery,
And today I am very happy with my new family.

I was in love with that man for many years,
And deep down inside me I still care.
It took me a while before I realized,
That our relationship was based on lies.
He was the love of my life,
But I did not get to be his wife.
Thankfully, he still plays his part as a father in our child's
life.

BROKEN PROMISES

He said that I was the love of his life,
And he promised, that I would be his wife.
'I will never cheat on you!' he said,
But it was not long before he had someone else in his bed.

He promised to be there whenever I needed him.
However, two months elapsed and I have not seen him.
He promised to love me no matter what,
But those words, were just another part of his act.

I thought that I was the only love in his life,
Yet, he had taken another woman to be his wife.
I was devastated and distraught,
For all those broken promises, led to a broken heart.

IN LOVE WITH A MARRIED MAN

I was tired of being used and abused by my lover
So I ended the relationship and looked for another.
On my thirty-first birthday
I held the party at Montego Bay,
There I was introduced to the most handsome man.
But unfortunately, he was someone else's husband.

Captivated by his muscular build and beauty,
I fell in love with him instantly.
Although I knew that he had a wife
I was desperate to be a part of his life.
I pursued him vigorously,
And seduced him until he made love to me.

We were like magnet and steel,
However, I could not let our little affair be revealed.
I loved him deeply
So I decided to have his baby.
But when I told him about the pregnancy
He became very angry with me.

He wanted me to have an abortion,
But I went against his decision
Which put him in a rather difficult position.
However, he handled the situation perfectly
And accepted his responsibility.
It was my greatest joy
The day I birthed our baby boy.

Everything was just as I wanted it to be.
But will he really leave his wife for me?
No, that was not to be.
For twenty years I was a part of that man's life
Yet, I could not convince him to leave his wife.

My life became a complete mess.
I was tired of being second best
So, I gave that lifestyle a permanent rest.
And today I am a Christian with a wonderful fiancé
Who loves and care for me dearly.

HOME ALONE

You were home alone and free. Free, Free.
Free from the children who had kept you so busy.
Free from their voices that would scream
Mummy, where is my frock?
Mummy, where are my socks?

Free from the anger in your husband's voice
As he shouted above the noise,
I am still waiting on that damn shirt,
Do not tell me I'm going to be late again for work!

Free from the difficult time you had.
As you struggled to keep the children in line,
You shuffled around the house
trying to do twenty things at the same time.
Free from the anger you felt at the tone of your husband's
voice
and all the various commotion and noise.

Now you are free to do things that before you could not get
done.
You are no longer annoyed with your husband
Who sits on the sofa with a newspaper in his hand,
Asking for beer, one by one.

The children are grown and have left home.
Your husband is at work and you are alone.
You feel free, free as a bird.
No children, grandchildren or husband to utter a word.

Free to relax from the stress
Which almost led to mental illness.

Now when the chores are finished you realised
That there is nothing else to keep you occupied.
You then decide to invite a friend or two
Unfortunately, the names that came to mind
Lived hundreds of miles from you.

Like clockwork the door opened, and your husband appeared
But it was not too long before he again, disappeared.
'Honey I will be back soon' he said,
But when he returned, you were already in bed.
The warmth of his body filled you with so much joy,
That you did not want to spend the following day
like a kid without a toy.

Being home alone was not as much fun as you expected,
Instead you became bored and frustrated.
So you then decided to set goals for your life,
Instead of being the lonely housewife.
Going back to school was an option
With the opportunity to further your education.
So you took advantage of the whole situation
and enrolled for courses of all description.

WHERE IS HE?

Where is the man who would listen and understand?
The man who would correct me when I'm wrong.
Where is the man who is loving and caring?
The man who called me honey, sometimes darling.
Where is he?

Where is the man who would comfort me when I am sad?
The man who is my children's dad.
Where is the man who took me for long walks in the park?
The man who shared my laughter and captured my heart.
Where is he?

Where is the man whose nearness increases the beating of
my heart?
The man who is so close and yet so far apart.
Where is the man who filled my heart with joy?
And made me feel like a little kid with a new toy.
Where is he?

Where is the man that I love so much?
That my body trembled at his touch.
Where is the man in whose arms I feel so comfortable and
secure?
That if he returns, I need not ask for anything more.
Where is he?

Where is my husband, lover and best friend?
Is our marriage coming to an end?
I have missed that man so much!

And I would like that man to get back in touch.
Because the man that I am seeing today,
Is not the same man I knew yesterday.
So where is he?

THE PHONE CALLS

I was loved and treated like a wife
And was very comfortable with my life.
My husband promised that we would spend the day in bed,
But he got a phone call and left instead.

A few days later
I asked him to do me a favour.
Unfortunately, he did not have any time.
But it was not too long after he got a phone call,
And again, I was left behind.

I don't know what I had done or said
For him to lose interest in me, especially in bed.
Apart from an occasional kiss
He acted as if I did not exist.
I was that man's wife
But there didn't seem to be much room for me in his life.

For fifteen years I was a part of his life,
Ten of which I was his wife.
But it seems as if his love for me had died,
And I could not figure out how it happened, or why.
However, I was taken by surprise
When I found out that an ex-lover was back in his life.

We drifted further apart day by day.
So then, I decided not to stay.
I had forgiven him too many times,
And was tired of all the lies.
So, I left to live my own life
Rather than being a part of his as his wife.

LOVE AT FIRST SIGHT

About fifteen years ago
I fell in love with a beautiful ewe.
It was love at first sight,
But I was not comfortable when I saw another ram at her side.
As I grazed with the flock in the field,
I was jealous of him who protects her like a shield.
I was desperate to catch a glimpse of any part of her that was reveal.

I was helplessly in love with her,
But I did not know if he was her brother or lover.
So, day by day I worked on a plan
On how to distract that other ram.
Finally I made a decision
That would supply answers to my questions.

As I walked with my sister towards the ewe,
I was confident that she would distract that other fellow.
But as we approached them he thought for a fact,
that they were on the verge of an attack.
My sister saw the rage in his eyes
And immediately, she came up with a little white lie.

Good afternoon sir. I hurt my foot at the pond.
Can you please lend a helping hand?
Captivated by her beauty and the melody of her voice,
He was helpless in making any other choice.

However, when she found out that he was the ewe's brother,
Her foot was no longer a bother.
I was very proud of the way my sister acted,
For she really did keep that other ram distracted.
I finally got the chance to meet the love of my life,
Who became the mother of my children, and my wife.

AN ORNAMENT

He pursued me until I became his wife.
But after the honeymoon he took a different turn in life.
A few years later I began to wonder,
Was he the same man I married, or was he another?

He gave me all kinds of material things in life,
but all I ever wanted was to be treated as his wife.
For all those things are just luxury,
and they can neither hear, feel, talk nor see.
Neither can they walk to bring me a cup of tea.

I was like an ornament on a shelf,
and I literally had to cry for help.
But he was not there.
So he could not hear.

Then someone pass by and heard my cry,
he took me down from the shelf,
and wiped the tears from my eyes.
Could my husband not see
how much he was hurting me?
Why could not someone
other than his best friend, rescue me?

However, one thing led to another,
and his best friend became my lover.
But, do not dare point a finger at me,
For he took me out of my misery.

NOT ONCE BUT TWICE

I had broken up with my daughter's mother.
When I fell in love with Zelia
Mistakenly, I thought that I had found the perfect partner.
For she was not the kind of person
that I thought she would be;
From the onset cheated on me.

They both said that I was a wonderful lover and dad.
So what have I done that was so bad?
I helped them cook, clean and do the laundry.
I even helped to take care of our baby.
So why did they both cheat on me?

I would go clubbing a few nights a week,
But that should not be a reason for them to cheat.
Women! They are so darn difficult to please.
But without one, my life seems incomplete.

Both ladies really did conquer my heart,
But we eventually grew apart.
Because once a cheater always a cheater,
And I prefer to do without either of them as a partner.
Today my children and I are living together.

AT THIS CRITICAL STAGE

There are so many difficulties I face each day,
I struggle to keep up
With the increasing pace along the way.
My whole life is falling apart before my eyes,
But at this critical stage it is no surprise.
Piece by piece it is stripped away,
As I stare helplessly in dismay.

There are no answers to be found,
Only numerous questions floating around.
Each day I look, and I see,
All the horrible things that happened to me.
The things that I hold so dear,
Others destroy and do not even care.

What if life is not what it should?
Does it have to be as bad as it is?
I try so hard to make it good,
But things never turn out as they should.

I find it hard to go from day to day.
It is as though it goes from bad to worse
without delay.
Yet I will fight the good fight day by day
And hope to see the light along the way.
Until then I will sit tight,
And try to enjoy my long and bumpy flight.

TO MY SURPRISE

You told me that you had broken up with your lover.
When we fell in love and moved in together,
You reassured me that the relationship was over.
But to my surprise, you were secretly seeing each other.

You turned down my proposal and I did not know why.
At that moment, I felt like I would die.
About two months later
I found out that you had left the country with your ex-lover.
When you left without our child,
I did not expect that you would treat us so unkind.

Now that he has taken another woman to be his wife,
You return with the expectation to come back into my life.
Well, my dear, I'm wiser and stronger.
I am just another ex-lover added to your number.

Four years ago you disappeared out of our lives.
There were no letters or notes to know if you were still alive.
So, my dear, I have moved on with my life,
and I have other children and a wonderful wife.

My darling dear, you really did conquer my heart,
But you had also broken it into many different parts.
I would not deprive our child of any visitation,
But please do not abuse the situation.
A man will forgive, but he will never forget,
Especially when he was not shown much love nor respect.

THE ACACIA TREE

An acacia tree was planted long ago,
Without any good soil or water for it to grow.
It was struggling to survive at the side of the road,
But was rescued by a loving soul.

The tree was grateful for the care,
It was glad that its life was spared.
Lots of water and nourishment it got,
As it blossomed and governed its patch.

The tree grew too big and strong,
So its rescuer decided to cut it down.
A stranger was paid to have it removed,
And it was not too long before it was doomed.

Again, it was struggling to survive,
And an old friend helped it to revive.
But its heart was still full of love,
For his first rescuer above.

She was the first love of his life,
whom he intended to be his wife.
He was willing to forgive her but found it hard,
So he laid a trap, and in it he fell.

The old friend had fallen in love with him,
and she decided to take him in.
He then was trapped between the two,
And knows not which one he should be married to.

AN APOLOGY

The day I saw you on the beach in that leopard colour bikini,
I fell in love with you instantly.
As the months passed we talked about having a family,
But I never thought that it would happen so quickly.
When I notice your belly begin to expand,
Reality kicked in and panic struck.
I then decided to take a hike,
Because I did not want to get stuck.

However, when I reached my final destination,
I realised that I had made the wrong decision.
I took up a note pad and a pen,
But I was too scared to write to you then.
You must have called me all kinds of horrible names,
And if I were in your shoes I would have probably done the
same.
Darling please forgive me for what I have done,
I have acted like a child and not as a man.

I know now that I should have shouldered my responsibility,
And take care of you and our baby.
My dear sweetheart, I really loved you,
And deep down in my heart I still do.
However, I am a shame to ask but, I will anyway.
'Did you give our baby away?'

FORGIVEN

I was not ready to start a family
But I would have done almost anything, to make you happy.
So I have decided to have your baby.
However, during my second trimester
You developed cold feet of becoming a father,
And my life was a total disaster.

I was also scared about the whole situation,
But I could not run away from my condition.
As I struggled to survive with my expanding tummy,
I often wondered if you would come back to me.
I even visualised us being together as a family.
But as the years passed I knew it was not going to be.

Sweetheart you were the first love of my life.
I honestly thought that I would become your wife.
But I was young and naive
And a lot of things I did believe.
I finally saw the light
And moved on with my life.

Nevertheless, I forgave you for what you have done,
But it does not mean that what you did, was not wrong.
You said you still love me and I love you too.
But do not let those three little words fool you,
Because I am not in love with you.
I did not give our child away
So you are welcome to visit her any day.

THE INVITATION

Thank you very much for the invitation,
But I hope it will not put you in a difficult position.
I can hardly wait to see my daughter.
I will do my very best to be a good father,
So do not worry too much about me.
I will not run away again, from my responsibility.

JUST BE THERE

I have already spoken to my children and husband.
We all agreed it was the best decision,
So you are not putting me in a difficult position.
I have had my daughter's best interest at heart,
And ten years are too far in the past
For me to keep malice that long in my heart.
I just want you to be there for our daughter,
Because she would like to know her biological father.

A DIFFERENT COLOUR

I fell in love with a handsome fellow.
All because of his race and colour,
My parents were against us being together.
We were broken hearted as we tried to stay apart,
From the relationship which had a great start.
Our emotions were intense
As we struggled to bring the intimate part to an end.
I could not let my parents know
That I was still seeing that handsome fellow.

I became depressed
And could no longer cope with the situation.
Unfortunately, I went in the wrong direction
And refused to believe that using drugs
would lead to an addiction.
When I realised what they meant
I was at a Rehabilitation Centre in Kent.
I probably would not have been sent there,
If my parents did not interfere
In our relationship that was so loving and sincere.

When we got engaged my parents were scared to interfere,
Because they did not want to lose their only daughter
Who was so precious and dear.
They accepted him
Even though he has a different colour skin.

For to be born of a different race is not a sin.
Today I am very happy with my family,
And I am looking forward to
my tenth wedding anniversary.

WAS IT BECAUSE I AM BLACK?

They were in the canteen drinking tea.
As I entered the room they all stared at me.
I smiled and said good morning,
But no one answered me.
Why did they look at me like that?
Was it because I am black?

The expression on their faces
Made me believe that they were racist.
I felt then like I wanted to run
far away from this place.
Run as if I was in a race.

Instead I stood there and stared,
As I struggled to fight back the tears.
Then I slowly put one foot in front of the other
And walked nervously towards a table in the far corner.

A woman of my colour and culture came and sat beside me.
I felt like I was rescued by the Holy Mary.
We sat there and discuss the matter,
Both agreeing that they hated the people, not the colour.

As a matter of fact,
At cocktail and dinner parties,
The majority always chose to wear the colour, Black.
So if they believed that black looks beautiful
with the colour of their skin,
Why on God's earth some of them think

That to be born black is a sin?

We are all made of flesh and blood,
And were created by the one true God
Who guides and protects us with his love.
There was darkness before light,
But some would say black before white.
However, it does not mean
That we must quarrel and fight.

It does not matter to which ethnic group,
religion or colour you belong,
We can live together as family and get along.
There is no need for racism or hypocrisy,
Just peace, love and unity.

WE ARE ONLY HUMAN

We are celebrities.
Some of our fans seem to think that we are flawless,
But only God Almighty, is perfect.
We may be talented and wealthier
but none of us is better than the other.
However, we are under a lot of pressure
As we try to please the media.
Sometimes we do go a bit haywire,
But you must not copy the wild behaviour.

Each of us is someone's mentor.
We have either a husband, a wife, a child or a lover.
If we get a divorce or part from a lover,
It becomes a big issue for the media.
Remember, we are human beings
With emotions and needs.
No one can really understand
The depths of one's emotions,
Unless he is in the same situation.

Our private life is an open book for everyone to see,
because of the media and the paparazzi.
If you had our talent and skills,
You would probably be in the same situation.
Then, you would realise it can drive one into depression.
To all our friends and fans,
Forgive us for whatever we have done that is wrong,
For we are only human.

AT WORK

There were circuit boards to be cleaned,
masked, varnished and demasked.
Some needed double varnishing and that was an extra task.
I always complained when I had to do the double varnishing,
But my supervisor was very understanding.
Sometimes he told me to just do the masking.

My dearest supervisor and friends,
Our working relationship has reached its end.
Unfortunately, my work there was temporary
And I have enjoyed working at the factory.
Varnishing was not my cup of tea,
But I did a very good job and have done it professionally.

I am very comfortable in my new job.
I have not regretted accepting it,
Despite the fact that sometimes I hardly have time to sit.
With all the stairs I have to climb I will probably keep fit.
So it saved me from purchasing an exercise kit.

New friends I have made at my present job,
But I have not forgotten the two best friends I ever had.
Izareen and Ian were very friendly.
I will always remember them wherever I may be.

THE STORE

The employees at the store are very helpful and friendly
And have tried their endeavor best to keep it tidy.
Excuse them for the boxes that are in the hall
and against the walls,
For there is not a large enough storeroom to keep them all.
That has put them in a very difficult position
I hope that in the future they would improve the situation.

Whenever you shop at the store
You are tempted to buy more and more.
Their prices are much lower
Than those of its competitors.
Have no fear in spending your money
For quality and quantity, is a certainty.

Also by the author

ISBN: 978-7456-224-3

9 781835 381762